JERUSALEM

SKYLINE

You ask for the number of gates
in Jerusalem, I count seven
Gates which are open to you, four
Gates sealed to me, and the Golden
Gate for the messiah who tarries.

DAVID ROKAH, VELO BA YOM AHER
And He Did Not Come Another Day

SKYLINE

JERUSALEM

DUBY TAL   MONI HARAMATI

MOD PUBLISHING HOUSE

JERUSALEM
SKYLINE
DUBY TAL, MONI HARAMATI

Photography: Duby Tal
Piloting: Moni Haramati
Photographs on pp. 57, 74, 143, 156, 221: David Netah
Produced by: Albatross Aerial Photography

Editing: Varda Raz, Duby Tal

Design and Supervision: Varda Raz

Research: Yoram Teharlev, Ruti Nahmani
Production Chief: Shalom Zadok

English Translation: Shmuel Himelstein
English Proofreading: David Grossman

Typesetting: El Ot Ltd.
Color Separation: Scanley Ltd.
Plates and Printing: Kal Press 1985 Ltd.
Printed in Israel 1994

Film Processing: Studio M, Jeffrey, Orient

Seventh edition - 2000

The authors wish to thank Meir Shalev, David Kroyanker,
Baruch Gian, Shmuel Haramati and Miriam Zlatkis for their
assistance in producing this book.

SOURCES

David Rokah, Velo Ba Yom Aher (And He Did Not Come Another Day), Dagah Publications
Benjamin of Tudela, Sefer HaMasa'ot (Itinerary) (1170), Sifriyat HaPoalim

SHA'AR HAGAI – GATEWAY TO THE VALLEY   14
LaPierre-Collins, Oh, Jerusalem!, Weidenfeld & Nicholson
Dudu Barak, Halil HaEtzem HeHalul (A Flute in the Hollow Bone), Shloshim Onot Shel Geshem (Thirty Seasons of Rain), Sifriyat HaPoalim
Simon Halkin, Yerushalayim, New York (Jerusalem, New York?), Poems, Sifriyat HaPoalim
Tuvia Rubner, Even Rotzeh Lizrom (Stone Wants to Flow), Ir Zot Ein Lehasig (This City Cannot be Obtained), Sifriyat HaPoalim
Amoz Oz, Micha'el Sheli (My Michael), Am Oved

JAFFA GATE   32
Psalm 122
Doron Rosenblum, Sha'alu Shlom Tugat Yerushalayim (Seek the Peace of Jerusalem's Grief), Hadashot
Dan Pagis, Ir HaTamid (City of Eternity), She'on HaTzel (Shadow Clock), Sifriyat HaPoalim
S.Y. Agnon, Lifnim min HaHomah (Inside the Wall), Schocken
Henry Baker Tristram, Travels in Palestine, Diary, 1863-1864

ZION GATE   70
David Shahar, Yom HaRefa'im (The Day of the Spirits), Am Oved
Amoz Oz, Micha'el Sheli (My Michael), Am Oved
Selma Langerloff, Yerushalayim, (Jerusalem) Jaffa, Sifriyah Hakla'it, 5681 (1921)

DUNG GATE   90
Nahmanides' prayer on the ruins of Jerusalem, Lu'ah Yerushalayim, 1949
A.B. Yehoshua, Mar Mani (Mr. Mani), HaSifriyah HaHadashah, HaKibbutz HaMe'uhad
Amoz Oz, Micha'el Sheli (My Michael), Am Oved
Henry Baker Tristram, Travels in Palestine, Diary, 1863-1864
Saul Bellow, To Jerusalem and Back, Idanim

GOLDEN GATE   120
Yitzhak Navon, Sheshet Hayamim VeShivat HaShe'arim (The Six Days and the Seven Gates)
Yitzhak Shalev, Al Gag HaNoter Dam (From the Roof of Notre Dame), Kolot Enosh Hamim (Warm Human Voices), Kiryat Sefer
Meir Shalev, Esav (Esau), Am Oved
S.Y. Agnon, T'mol Shilshom (Yesterday and the Day Before), Schocken
Mota Gur, Har HaBayit Beyadeinu (The Temple Mount is in our Hands), Ministry of Defence Publications
Mark Twain, The Innocents Abroad, 1867, Levinson
Ahad HaAm, Lifnei HaKotel (Before the Wall), Devir
Hayyim Beer, Notzot (Feathers), Am Oved
Theodor Herzl, Hazon Yerushalayim (Vision of Jerusalem), Lu'ah Yerushalayim, 1950

LIONS' GATE   142
Haim Guri, Ir Petza (Wound City), HaKibbutz HaMe'uhad
Italo Calvino, HeArim HaSemuyot MeiAyin (The Cities Hidden from the Eye)
Meir Shalev, Esav (Esau), Am Oved
Haim Guri, Dapei Yerushalayim (Jerusalem Pages), Hakibbutz HaMe'uhad
Yoram Teharlev, Givat HaTahmoshet (Ammunition Hill), Ministry of Defence Publications
Speech of Yitzhak Rabin marking 25 years after the liberation of Jerusalem

HEROD'S GATE   164
Yehudah Halevi, Yefeh Nof
David Ben-Gurion, Tifarta shel Yerushalayim (The Glory of Jerusalem)
Levin Kipnis, Yonim Shtayim (Doves Two), Mifgashim, Am Oved
Yehudah Amihai, Poem 21 of a Series on Jerusalem, Schocken
Meir Shalev, Hayeled Hayyim VeHaMifletzet MiYerushalayim (The Child Hayyim and the Monster from Jerusalem), HaKibbutz HaMe'uhad

DAMASCUS GATE   186
Mark Twain, The Innocents Abroad
S.Y. Agnon, Kenagan HaMenagen (As a Musician Playing), Schocken
Maimonides, Laws of Fasts, Chapter 8: 12-13
Yehoash Biber, Arafel Boker Yerushalayim (Morning Fog Jerusalem), Memorial Volume

NEW GATE   206
From a speech by Teddy Kollek, November 4, 1992
Aviad Forheles, sport column, Yedi'ot Aharonot, November 15, 1992
David Ben-Gurion, Tifarta shel Yerushalayim (The Glory of Jerusalem)

CLOSING GATE   232
Elsa Lasker-Schueller, Jerusalem, Land of the Hebrews, Moznayim 57, August 31, 1984
Yosef Sarig, Or Virushalayim (Light and Jerusalem), Ministry of Defence Publications
Yehoash Biber, Aharei Preidah (After Parting), Memorial Volume, Yehoash Biber

. . . And from there to Jerusalem, a small, fortified town nesting behind three walls, with a large number of people –
Ishmaelites, Jacobites, Armenians, Georgians and Franks – speaking every foreign tongue. The dyeing concession is
bought each year by the Jews from the king, so that no person in the town except the Jews may engage in dyeing.
There are about two hundred Jews, who live beneath David's Tower at the edge of the town. Inside the wall of David's
Tower is a building whose foundation extends about ten cubits, this being part of an ancient building which our
forefathers built, while the rest was built by the Ishmaelites. There is no stronger place in the entire town than
David's Tower.

There are two buildings there, the first being le Hospital, which is both an inn and a hospital, from which
four hundred horsemen ride out. This is where all the sick people come. There they are supplied with all that they
need, both while alive and after death.

The second building is referred to as "Solomon's Temple," that being the palace which King Solomon – peace
be upon him – constructed. That is where the horsemen dwell, and each day three hundred of them emerge to wage
battle, excluding the horsemen who hail from France and from Edom. These have all taken a vow to remain there for
a year or for a number of years, until the end of the period of their vows.

There one also finds the Great Church, where lies buried that man whose grave all the erring Christians visit.

There are four gates in Jerusalem: Abraham's Gate, David's Gate, Zion Gate, and Jehoshaphat's Gate, the
latter opposite where the Temple used to be in ancient times. Omar ibn el-Khattab built a large and most magnificent
dome upon that site. The Gentiles do not bring any statue or likeness into it, but merely come to recite their prayers
there. Before it stands the Western Wall, one of the walls which used to be in the Holy of Holies, and it is known as
the Gate of Mercy. The Jews all come to pray in the courtyard before the Wall.

In Jerusalem, in Solomon's House, is the horse stable which he built, a very strong building constructed of
large rocks. There is no other building to compare with it in the entire country. To this day one can see there the pool
where the priests would offer their sacrifices. Those who come there from Judea write their names on the wall. When
one leaves Jehoshaphat's Gate to enter the Valley of Jehoshaphat, he is already in the desert. There one finds Yad
Avshalom – the memorial to Avshalom – and the grave of King Uzziah. There is also a large spring there, with the
waters of the Shilo'ah in Nahal Kidron. Above the spring is a building from the days of our forefathers, but there is
very little water in the spring. As to the people of Jerusalem, most drink rainwater which they keep in barrels in their
homes. One ascends from the Valley of Jehoshaphat to the Mount of Olives, for Jerusalem and the Mount of Olives are
both but one valley. From the Mount of Olives one can see the Sea of Sodom. From the Sea of Sodom is a distance of
two parsangs (i.e., about eight miles – trans.) to the Pillar of Salt, which was Lot's wife. The cattle lick at it, but it is
always restored to what it was. Before Jerusalem lie three Jewish cemeteries, where they would bury their dead in
those days. Each tombstone had a date on it, but the Edomites destroyed the graves and built homes from the
tombstones.

BENJAMIN OF TUDELA, SEFER HAMASA'OT
(Itinerary) (1170)

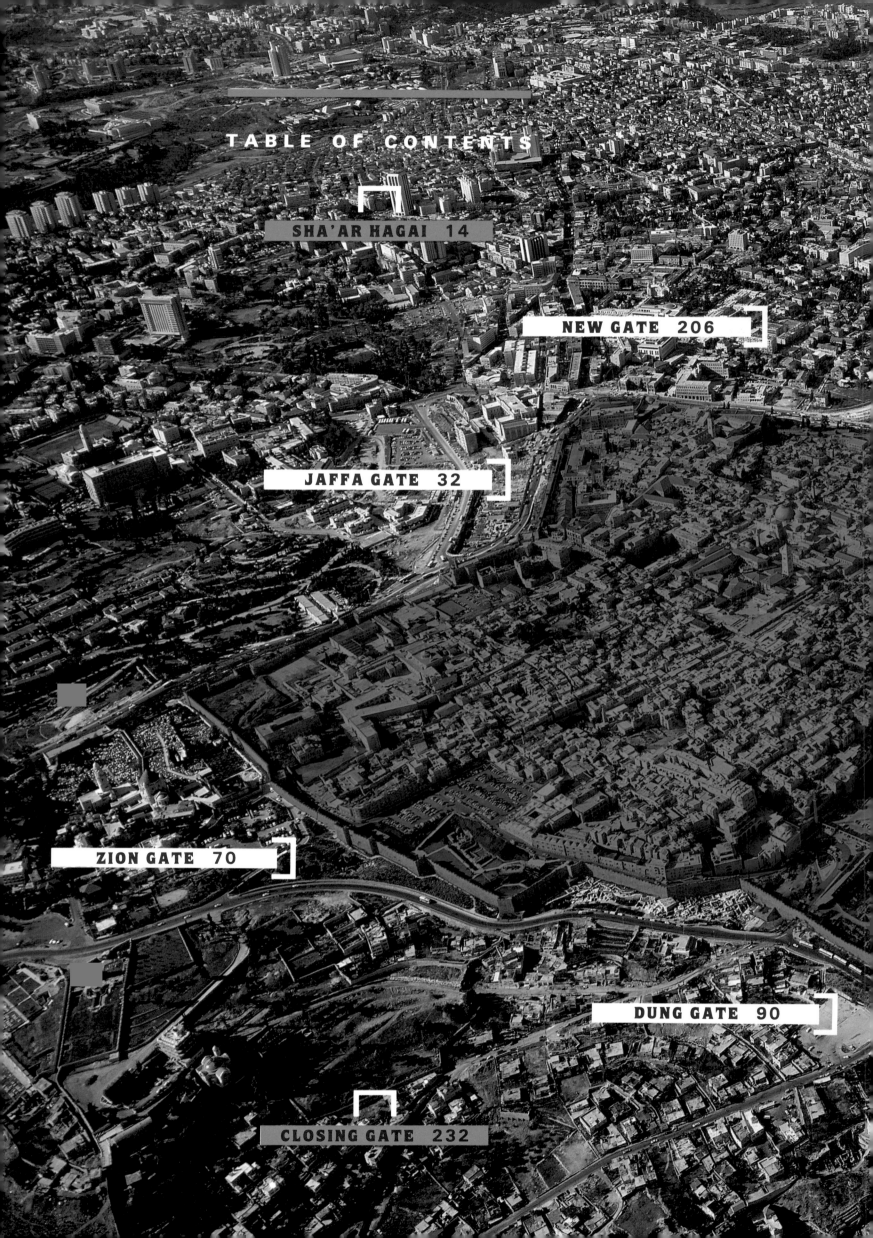

TABLE OF CONTENTS

DAMASCUS GATE   186

HEROD'S GATE   164

LIONS' GATE   142

GOLDEN GATE   120

SHA'AR HAGAI

GATEWAY TO THE VALLEY

. . . From there, for twenty miles, the road twisted its way up a series of tight curves, its path buried at the foot of the valley, each of its sides a sheer, impenetrable descent of rock and forest. There every rock could hide a rifleman, every curve an ambush, every clump of trees a company of attackers. Even the communities dominating from their rocky perches the valley floor were in Arab hands: Kastel, hugging its heights by the ruins of a Crusader castle built in its turn upon the Roman fort that guarded the western approach to Jerusalem in Christ's time; Abu Ghosh, where David had kept the Ark of the Covenant for two decades waiting to enter Jerusalem; Kolonia, rest area for Titus' legionnaires during the siege of Jerusalem.

It was not until the road had reached the heights of the Judean plateau and the kibbutz of Kiryat Anavim that a Jewish traveller could feel safe again. Four miles farther on, the road crested up to its culminating point. There, at the end of a long left-hand curve, the suburbs of Jerusalem promised safety at last.

Successors to the camel caravans of Biblical times, the chariots of the Romans, the zealous columns of the Crusades, wheezing lines of Jewish trucks and buses now struggled up that gulch to Jerusalem, carrying in their vans the ingredients vital for the city's life. Protecting that fragile communication line was an immense, almost insurmountable problem.

LARRY COLLINS & DOMINIQUE LAPIERRE, O JERUSALEM!

Nehemiah mentions that he began his trip to the city from Sha'ar HaGai. The name refers to a site on the way to Jerusalem. The Hebrew name Sha'ar HaGai is a translation of the Arabic Bab el Wad, the Valley Gate, which leads to Jerusalem.

And if we find the hollowed-bone flute

and we say that the Levites have beat out its rhythm

and yet they said its voice issued from the house

of David

and then wasn't it just as it had once been

Already the overlords across the river won't recite

psalms of praise

perhaps the overlords across the river said

what they said

but as if in space today, its vaunted song

trembles no more

and if it'll tremble it won't be from David's mouth

bearing witness

It's years that I haven't heard flutes in the valley

and violins hung up afar and fallen silent by the

river

like a flute

like a violin

like the weeping that has ceased

And if we find the hollow-bone flute

and if ever I were David, son of Yishai

and if ever –

the day has come

now I am Shaul

who was taken from the argent

from the golden.

DUDU BARAK, HALIL HAETZEM HEHALUL
(A Flute in the Hollow Bone)
Translated by Aloma Halter

BEIT ZEIT RESERVOIR, west of Jerusalem
used for storing winter flood waters

Only in Jerusalem might a person

Lose his composure over a sudden morning's snow.

SIMON HALKIN, YERUSHALYIM, NEW YORK?
(Jerusalem, New York?)

THE EIN HEMED INTERCHANGE

THE EIN HEMED (AQUA BELLA) INTERCHANGE.

The approach of Jerusalem from the west.

THE MA'ALEH ADUMIM REGION,

on the Jerusalem-Jericho Road, east of Jerusalem

WHERE THE JUDEAN HILLS AND THE COASTAL PLAIN MEET

northwest of Jerusalem

Stone wants to flow

olive tree wishes to become stone

churches ask their hearts to fly

a cloud perches on the Temple Mount

suns wandered out of doors, became thorns

wars passed over her – dreams

shadows come and go with radiant faces

her silence is bells upon bells

stones flow

the olive tree is stone

the one who sleeps with his heart awake, knows at night

that this heavy city rises to sail in the moon

TUVIA RUBNER, EVEN ROTZEH LIZROM
(Stone Wants to Flow)
Translated by Aloma Halter

THE APPROACH TO JERUSALEM FROM THE EAST

23

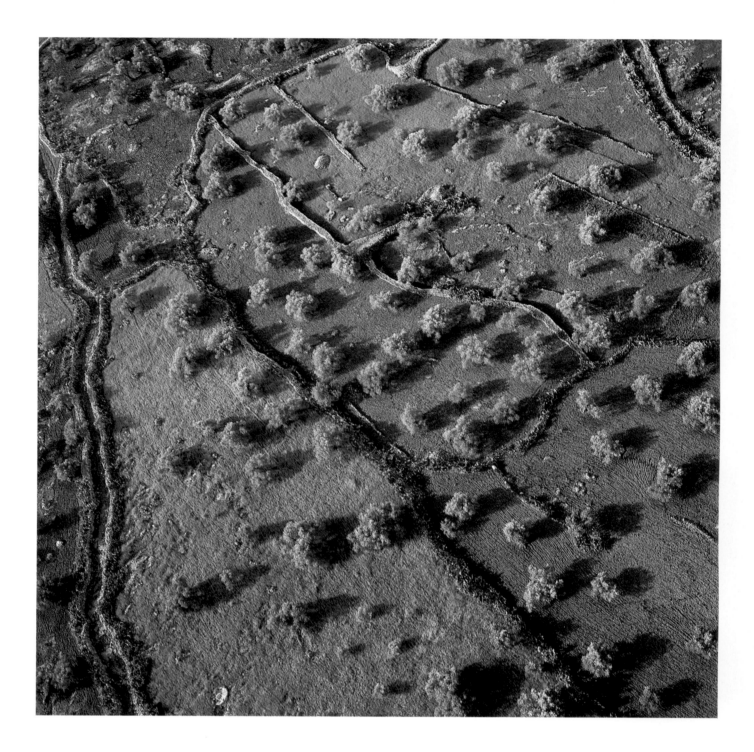

OLIVE GROVES IN THE JUDEAN HILLS

NAHAL SHMUEL, a seasonal watercourse, near Ramot, named after the Prophet Samuel (view southward)

THE JUDEAN HILLS, NORTH OF KIBBUTZ MA'ALEH HAHAMISHAH AND NATAF SETTLEMENT

THE JERUSALEM – TEL AVIV HIGHWAY, on the left side is ABU GHOSH, A MUSLIM ARAB VILLAGE

27

THE GIV'AT ZE'EV – RAMOT ROAD, NEAR NEBI SAMWIL ("PROPHET SAMUEL"),
where, according to Byzantine sources, the prophet Samuel is buried

THE TRAIN TO JERUSALEM, THE NAHAL SOREQ ROUTE
a seasonal watercourse from the Judean foothills to the Mediterranean

29

. . . At the foot of the slope in the German Colony gradient in the south of Jerusalem a weary train is climbing. The engine howls and pants. It collapses into the arms of the deserted platforms. The last puff of steam escapes with a helpless wheeze. One last time the engine bellows against the silence. But the silence is too strong. The engine surrenders, succumbs, grows cold. Sabbath eve. A vague expectancy. Even the birds are silent. His feet are standing perhaps in the gates of Jerusalem.

AMOS OZ, MICHA'EL SHELI
(My Michael)

THE JERUSALEM RAILWAY STATION
The railway station was built at the end of the 19th century, to serve the increasing number
of pilgrims traveling to Jerusalem

JAFFA GATE

A song of degrees of David: I rejoiced when they said to me,

"Let us go to the House of the Lord."

Our feet stood within your gates, O Jerusalem.

Jerusalem is built as a city which is knit together.

Where the tribes, the tribes of the Lord – the testimony of Israel –

go up to give thanks to the name of the Lord.

For there stood thrones of judgment, the thrones of the house of David.

Pray for the peace of Jerusalem; may those who love it prosper.

Peace be within your walls, tranquility within your palaces.

For my brethren's and companions' sakes, I will now say, "Peace be within you."

Because of the house of the Lord our God I will seek your good.

PSALM 122

This gate is the principal entrance to the Old City.
Its name in Arabic is Bab-el-Khalil, the gate of Hebron, as the main road to Hebron started here.
It was also called Jaffa Gate because the road to Jaffa and the coast also started from it.

. . . In short, I pray that the policeman in the patrol car stationed permanently at the only entrance to Jerusalem will order you to turn around and return to Tel Aviv, for you are not Jewish enough, not nationalistic enough, not traditional enough, not political enough, not involved enough, not touristy enough, not identified enough with someone or something, to just casually enter Jerusalem.

But this still does not happen, and therefore please pave a path – you, the Eretz Israelites, the "cool," the "hip," the arrogant; owners of plastic baskets, carriers of egg cartons, who cross the worn-out buildings of skyscraperless Jaffa Road, of grimy walls; creatures of all kinds, of strong views, saturated with political, military and religious awareness, sellers of pickles, vendors of nibbles, various and sundry fearers of God, local heroes, holders of theories, humus experts – clear the way for the local post-Romantic tourist, the secularist lacerated by an infinity of cliches about Jerusalem, for whom Jerusalem no longer sets off chords, who knows that nothing good will come of Jerusalem, and who nevertheless still seeks to find some type of hint of the positive in spite of all in Jerusalem; clear the way for those who have been able to navigate all the curves, and even the police car, and who have reached the Binyanei HaUmah traffic light, and who generally don't know what to do with themselves, once they have finally reached Jerusalem.

DORON ROSENBLUM, SHA'ALU SHLOM TUGAT YERUSHALAYIM
(Seek the Peace of Jerusalem's Grief)

THE APPROACH TO THE CITY
AND THE OUTSKIRTS OF THE KIRYAT MOSHE NEIGHBORHOOD

THE MAIN APPROACH FROM THE WEST TO JERUSALEM

AGRIPPAS STREET

AGRIPPAS STREET AND THE NAHLA'OT AREA, view eastward

Run to and fro in the squares of Jerusalem, and see now, and know and seek in its streets.

THE MAHANEH YEHUDAH MARKET, the largest market in the New City
The area was named after Yehudah Navon. The market was established
in 1928 and has about 120 shops.

THE OHEL MOSHE NEIGHBORHOOD (foreground),
built between 1883 and 1885, with the help of the Mazkeret Moshe Fund,
established in 1874 in memory of Sir Moses (Moshe) Montefiore
AND THE MAHANEH YEHUDAH MARKET

JAFFA ROAD AND AGRIPPAS STREET, WITH THE PRODUCE MARKET
BETWEEN THE TWO; THE (FORMER) ALLIANCE ISRAELITE UNIVERSELLE
SCHOOL (constructed in 1899) AND THE CLAL CENTER

THE (FORMER) ALLIANCE VOCATIONAL SCHOOL
The building was constructed in 1899, with the aid of Baroness de Hirsch

A

Wounded from the psalms of praise
engraved by daggers
on her frail shoulders, crowned with a halo
of holy flames, all the legions
have swooped down on her seeking redemption
in her arms, have made her the world's epicenter
for all those demanding miracles, and sacrificed
and crucified her to the greater glory of her name
without stopping or wondering why
she hides herself behind wall upon wall.

B

City of Eternity, like a swarthy fist boxed-in
by stone, and still waiting – stiff-necked,
boundaried, constrained, to become as tranquil
as interlaced fingers.
But she's full with all the miracle workers,
the diviners expecting a sign
to fall from the heavens
that will transform her, burying her soul
in a handful of Holy Land grit, forever sanctifying it
beneath their feet, like a graveyard.

DAN PAGIS, IR HATAMID
(City of Eternity)
Translated by Aloma Halter

THE SUNDIAL ON JAFFA ROAD, The sundial was built in 1918
and was formerly used to determine prayer times

THE MEKOR BARUCH NEIGHBORHOOD, founded in 1924
The name was based on the verse (Proverbs 5:18),
"Let the fountain be Blessed" (Merkor Baruch in Hebrew)

. . . There are places in Jerusalem with which I am familiar and know about, and yet when I happen upon them it seems to me that I have never seen them before. Yet, in contrast, there are places where I have never been, and when I come there it seems to me that I am familiar with and know them.

And because I have always wandered the streets of Jerusalem by day and by night, I never had the time to learn any craft. Worse than that, I was not occupied with the study of the Torah, and a Jew who does not study the Torah is admonished by his heart: What will you say on the Day of Judgment when they ask you "Did you study Torah?" And what will I say? I will say that I studied Jerusalem, and I am certain that they will say to me – "You have done well." And it seems to me that the words that I have prepared as an answer for the Day of Judgment were acceptable to my heart as well, and it no longer chides me.

Sometimes my heart even wandered about with me from place to place and rejoiced with me – until I left Jerusalem and went to a foreign land and spent there all the days of the Great War and some years after, not by my own volition, until the Almighty brought me back to my place, to Jerusalem.

And because my soul overflowed that the Almighty had brought me back to my place and I could walk about Jerusalem as in the days of old, I broke forth with praise of the Lord and of Jerusalem, the city that the Almighty had selected of all His creation. Even though He exiled Himself, as it were, from her, He did not take away her uniqueness.

S.Y. AGNON, LIFNIM MIN HAHOMAH
(Inside the Wall)

SHA'AREI HESSED (founded in 1909) to the left
The neighborhood was built during the years 1909-1939 by the Sha'arei
Hessed General Philanthropic Association AND BATEI RAND to the right

THE NAHLA'OT NEIGHBORHOOD

46

THE KNESSET YISRAEL NEIGHBORHOOD (founded in 1891), BATEI BROIDE, BATEI RAND

ZION SQUARE, was named for the Zion Cinema which was the center of
cultural life in Jerusalem in the 1920s and 1930s, BANK HAPOALIM, (the
tall building), SANSUR BUILDING built in 1931 in European Style with
Rococo ornamentation

ZION SQUARE AND THE PEDESTRIAN MALL BEN-YEHUDAH STREET
Eliezer Ben Yehudah revived Hebrew as a spoken language, and lived
and worked in Jerusalem from 1880 to 1920

. . . This is an account of the anguish of Jerusalem in the past twenty years: at first, in the early 'Seventies, it was "In." The symbol of spontaneous hedonism at that time was "to take off for Jerusalem, just like that, in the middle of the night." It was then fashionable to compete in one's love for Jerusalem, to live in Nahla'ot, to spread out on an Arab carpet . . . A decade later, Jerusalem became so "Out," that many Jerusalemites only mentioned where they were from in the midst of a coughing spell.

It is true that there are objective reasons why the lustre of secular, Israeli, tangible Jerusalem has declined (hand-in-hand with the ascent of Jewish Peopleish, declarative, nationalistic Jerusalem), and there are certified statistics and research findings to this effect (the growth in the number of ultra-Orthodox, the limited number of jobs and opportunities for the young, modest purchasing power, the decline of the urban center because of the obsession with building new neighborhoods, etc. The latest study shows a demographic revolution, in which percentagewise there has been greater growth among the Jewish population than among the Arab population, thanks to the ultra-Orthodox. The flight of the secular also has a statistical basis) — but there is reason to suspect that some of these advances and declines in the status of secular "Jerusalem" are no more than journalistic inventions. Take the history of modern journalism — and you have an abridged version of Jerusalem's anguish, along with the abridged history of the Tel Aviv boom. Tel Aviv is but froth and vapor, which is taken seriously only by Jerusalem. It was Jerusalem which gave birth to the local press, which invented Tel Aviv, along with the conviction that Jerusalem was "Out." But, of course, one cannot tell what came first — the fact or the recognition of that fact. We all became localites, rejected by one another, and it is all wearisome.

It is so wearisome that we will only review it briefly, if only to sense in our bones the cliche-ridden anguish of Tel Aviv-Jerusalem: Tel Aviv is living it up, Tel Aviv is a note from your parents which releases you from the stigma of Zionism, of the strangehold of theocracy, of the armed community which we really are. In Jerusalem, all assumptions are nullified. Jerusalem's anguish is the anguish of the existence of the creature itself.

DORON ROSENBLUM, SH'ALU SHELOM TUGAT YERUSHALAYIM
(Seek the Peace of Jerusalem's Grief)

JERUSALEM CENTER, THE INTERSECTION OF JAFFA ROAD, KING GEORGE AND STRAUSS STREETS

JERUSALEM TOWER AND THE TRIANGLE (JAFFA ROAD – KING DAVID STREET, BEN-YEHUDAH STREET)

ME'AH SHE'ARIM AND BATEI UNGARN

THE GENERALI BUILD NG, WHERE JAFFA ROAD AND SHLOMZION HAMALKA STREET MEET

55

THE RELIGIOUS NEIGHBORHOODS IN THE NORTH OF THE CITY AND ME'AH
SHEARIM STREET. Me'ah Shearim was the fifth Jewish quarter to be
established outside the Old City, in 1874.
The name is derived from the Bible passage, "Then Isaac sowed in that
land, and received in the same year a hundredfold (Me'ah Shearim); and
the Lord blessed him" (Genesis 26:12)

FUNERAL OF THE RABBI OF GUR IN THE GEULAH NEIGHBORHOOD,
MALKHEI YISRAEL STREET

BATEI UNGARN – THE TRIANGULAR COURTYARD

The Batei Ungram (literally "Hungarian Houses") neighborhood was founded and built by Jews who came from Austria, Hungary and Bohemia

SABBATH SQUARE, OFF ME'AH SHEARIM, AT THE INTERSECTION OF STRAUSS AND MALKHEI YISRAEL STREETS

SCHNELLER TOWER, A HIGH GOTHIC CLOCK TOWER, part of a former
German Protestant complex which was built between 1856 and 1900.
The complex included an orphanage for children who had survived the
Massacre of Christians in Syria, in 1840.

WITH THE MEKOR BARUCH NEIGHBORHOOD IN THE BACKGROUND

THE BEIT YISRAEL NEIGHBORHOOD,
founded in 1887

. . . One new building, out of harmony with the other surroundings, arrested our attention – the immense Russian pile, which has arisen on the rising ground to the west of the city since my last visit, and which completely overshadows every other architectural feature. It combines in some degree the appearance and the uses of the cathedral close, public offices, barracks, and hostelry; the flag of the Russian Consulate floats over one part, while the tall cupola of the church commands the centre. There are many Russian priests and monks, and shelter is provided for the Muscovite pilgrims. Still the whole style of the group seems a sort of taking possession of the land by anticipation, in strong contrast with the simple and chaste cluster on the top of Mount Zion, where the English Mission has its centre. The Greeks view this Russian establishment with great jealousy, not to say dislike, and attribute it to a settled determination on the part of the Czar to separate the Muscovite Church altogether from the Greek, and throw off what little dependence is still acknowledged on the Patriarchate of Constantinople. They remark with some bitterness on the settlement of a Russian bishop in Jerusalem in addition to or rather in rivalry of the Greek Patriarch.

HENRY BAKER TRISTRAM, TRAVELS IN PALESTINE, DIARY, 1863-1864.

THE RUSSIAN CHURCH, THE RUSSIAN DELEGATION BUILDING, AND THE COURTS
This land (19 acres) belonged to the Russian Government. In the 1950's most was sold to the Israeli Government

THE RUSSIAN CHURCH AND THE NEW MUNICIPAL BUILDING – JANUARY 1992

THE RUSSIAN CHURCH AND THE NEW MUNICIPAL BUILDING – NOVEMBER 1992

You, son of man, take a tile, and place it before you, and trace upon it a city, Jerusalem.

EZEKIEL 4:1

THE MAMILLA PROJECT, an exclusive housing development,
near the walls of the Old City. Mamilla is an Arab word. Mamil'a =
MA-MIN-ALLAH – water from God; or, MA-AMEN-ALLA – with Trust in
God – three words that Arabs say at a burial service.

JAFFA ROAD AND THE CITY CENTER

ZION GATE

. . . The sun, on the verge of setting, bathed all — the Old City, its wall, the cries of
all its churches and domes, the Mount of Olives, Tur-Malka, the houses of the New
City and the clean blue sky, clear of any cloud in the bright and muted light.
The air became so lucid that everything began to throb. The sounds of crystal and
a feeling of happiness permeated me as if a good dream had been transformed into
reality, as if I had entered into a legendary castle, but at the same time I felt that the
castle had opened up within me, as if I were no longer a single child, a small creature
who peeks out at the world surrounding it, but on the contrary: all of Jerusalem,
with its surrounding hills, with the entire region which surrounds the hills and the skies,
all these are within me, and it is my body which surrounds them; they stem from
within it, and within it they exist.

DAVID SHAHAR, YOM HAREFA'IM
(The Day of the Spirits)

The western gate of the Old City named after Mount Zion.
In Arabic it is known as "the Prophet David's Gate," because one passes through it to King David's tomb on Mount Zion.

Fair its peak, pride of all the earth, Mount Zion, summit of the north.

PSALMS 48:3

THE WINDMILL IN YEMIN MOSHE. The windmill was built in 1857 by
Sir Moses Montefiore to grind flour and thus bring down its cost.
Montefiore was the man who was responsible for the expansion
of the early Jewish quarter beyond the walls of the Old City.

IN THE BACKGROUND LIE MOUNT ZION AND THE DORMITION ABBEY,
completed in 1910 for the Benedictine Catholic Order

THE WINDMILL – WITH THE BACKGROUND OF THE OLD CITY WALL
AND THE HEBREW UNIVERSITY ON MOUNT SCOPUS

KEREN HAYESOD STREET AND THE KING SOLOMON, MORIAH AND KING DAVID HOTELS

A VIEW FROM THE OLD CITY WALL OF MISHKENOT SHA'ANANIM, YEMIN MOSHE AND THE NEW CITY

Mishkenot Sha'ananim was the first neighborhood beyond the walls, built in 1860.

TERRA SANCTA COLLEGE AND KIKAR ZAREFAT (FRENCH SQUARE)
(INTERSECTION OF KEREN HAYESOD, GAZA AND AGRON STREETS)

EMEK REFA'IM STREET AND THE GERMAN COLONY
The name Refaim derived from the Bible (II Samuel 5:22) as the place
where the Philistines were defeated by King David.
THE GERMAN COLONY was built by German Templars at the end of 19th
century as an agricultural settlement. Their aim was to establish a small
"Kingdom of God" in Israel, with Jerusalem at its center.

on the left YESHURUN SYNAGOGUE AND RONDO CAFE,

on the right HEICHAL SHLOMO named for the father of the philanthropist

Sir Isaac Wolfson (home of the Chief Rabbinate),

AND THE SHERATON PLAZA HOTEL

KIKAR ZAREFAT AND KING GEORGE STREET

THE YMCA TOWER ON KING DAVID STREET

The building was designed by Q. L. Harmon, who designed New York's Empire State Building. It was completed in 1933.

The building has three main sections. The triangular motif expresses the aims of the Young Men's Christian Association:

The development of the body, the mind and the spirit

. . . There is no end to Jerusalem. Talpiot, a forgotten continent in the south, hidden among her ever-whispering trees. A bluish vapor spreads up from the Judean Desert which borders Talpiot to the east. The vapor touches her small villas, and even her gardens, overshadowed by the pines. Beit HaKerem, a solitary hamlet lost beyond the windswept plain, hemmed in by rocky fields. Bayit Vegan, an isolated hill-fort where a violin plays behind windows kept shuttered all day, and at night the jackals howl to the south. Tense silence broods in Rehavia, in Saadya Gaon Street, after the sun has set. At a lighted window sits a grey-haired sage at his work, his fingers tapping at the keys of his typewriter. Who could imagine that at the other end of this very street stands the district of Shaarei Hesed, full of barefoot women wandering at night between coloured sheets flapping in the breeze, and sly cats slipping from yard to yard? Is it possible that the old man playing tunes on his German typewriter cannot sense them? Who could imagine that beneath his western balcony spreads the Valley of the Cross, an ancient grove creeping up the slopes, clutching at the outermost houses of Rehavia as if about to enfold and smother them in its luxuriant vegetation? Small fires flicker in the valley, and long-drawn-out, muffled songs rise out of the woods and towards the window-panes.

AMOS OZ, MICHA'EL SHELI
(My Michael)

A TOWER DATING BACK TO THE OTTOMAN PERIOD IN THE RATISBONNE AREA (THE CITY CENTER)
The Ratisbonne Monastery was built by an apostate Jew of that name. Most of its land was sold off to builders

PRIVATE HOME ON HAMATZOR STREET, OLD KATAMON.

The name Katamon means "beside the Monastery," a reference to the monastery in the area

INTERSECTION OF ALKELAI AND YIZRE'ELI STREETS, TALBIEH,
a prestigious neighborhood, home to various consultates and public instituticns, including the President's Residence

THE CINEMATHEQUE, VALLEY OF BEN HINNOM AND SULTAN'S POOL
The Sultan's Pool was built by Suliman the Magnificent.

JERUSALEM SWIMMING POOL, EMEK REFA'IM STREET

85

SULTAN'S POOL BRIDGE AND MISHKENOT SHE'ANANIM

VALLEY OF BEN HINNOM AND MOUNT ZION HOTEL

87 The Valley of Ben Hinnon derived its name from the Bible. Joshua (15:8 18:16)

. . . It may happen, for example, that a person decides to conduct a tour of all of Jerusalem. He goes to the Jaffa Gate, turns left, arrives at the square and massive David's Tower, and wanders into the narrow alley which leads, alongside the wall, to the Zion Gate. Close to the wall is a Turkish barracks, from which one hears sounds of weapons and military music. Afterwards he passes by the large Armenian monastery, which stands firm as a fortress with strong walls and gates equipped with locks and bolts. A little further on one approaches a heavy, gray building, which is labelled "David's Tomb," and when one sees it he is aware that he is standing in the holy Zion, on the mountain of kings.

One cannot then but think that the entire mountain is but a single dome, on which King David sits with a gold scepter on a throne of fire and to this day holds his scepter over Jerusalem and Eretz Israel. He must think that the remnants of the wall, which cover the ground, are the remains of a king's fortress which fell, and that the ridge across the way is the messianic hill, where Solomon sinned, because the valley at which he is looking beneath him is the deep Valley of Gei-Hinnom, which was once filled with dead bodies, people killed in Jerusalem at the time it was destroyed by the Romans.

SELMA LANGERLOFF, YERUSHALAYIM
(Jerusalem)

THE DORMITION ABBEY ON MOUNT ZION
A modern church and monastery built between 1906 and 1910 and belonging to the Benedictine Order.
The octagonal church building is on the summit of Mount Zion.

DUNG GATE

... Our feet stood in your gates, O Jerusalem, the House of God and the Gate to Heaven. Jerusalem rebuilt is a city knit together with its inhabitants.

To it did the tribes – the tribes of God – ascend; in it stands the Foundation Stone of the universe, from which the world was formed.

From it were woven the foundations of the world and its borders. There stands Mount Moriah, from whence comes forth Torah and deliverance – the mountain which God desired for His dwelling place, where He built His resting place, and where He established the throne of His kingdom. There His dwelling and habitation are whole.

From the Temple it passes to the Holy of Holies, where stood the Tablets of the Covenant of the Master of the Universe, written with the finger of God. From there prophecy went forth, spreading to the deepest recesses of the soul. There the Cherubs spread their wings upon the chariot of those going out to do battle. Two roes that are twins are the creatures beneath the God of Israel in the River Kebar. I know that the Cherubs are both in the future and the past. Two visages does the Cherub have, inward and outward, with faces of justice and faces of goodwill, and the spirit of God in its wings.

The glory of the God of Israel is above them, a dwelling place for the divine presence; for there the Holy Temple is directed toward hearing the singing and the prayer.

PRAYER OF NAHMANIDES ON THE RUINS OF JERUSALEM

The Dung Gate is mentioned in the book of Nehemiah as a dispatch point for the city's refuse. It would appear that it was through this gate that the refuse was removed from the city.

THE OPHEL The northern part of the city of David
AND THE SOUTHERN WALL OF THE TEMPLE MOUNT

92

THE REMAINS OF A BYZANTINE MONASTERY IN MA'ALEH ADUMIM

ROMAN ERA RUINS NEAR THE HILTON HOTEL, dated to the Roman Period.

95

. . . What does it have to offer, Nothing much, Colonel. A single famous and striking mosque, the Dome of the Rock is its name, sir, and you have no doubt heard of it. A few important churches, foremost of them the Church of the Holy Sepulcher, which, if you don't mind my saying so, is especially disappointing. Preferable to it are the small churches outside the wall, which are all harmonious and pleasant. Whenever, sir, you feel a desire to tour, the Advocacy will send you an excellent guide.

— Half a day will certainly be enough, sir, to have a leisurely tour of all the holy places, for all are located one next to the other, and the distances are laughable, I almost said tragic.

— Beyond the walls, sir, are a number of new neighborhoods, spread out along hills, where just this frosty winter I found a number of corners to which one can become attached, but in order to understand their spell, I think, sir, that a certain amount of time has to elapse.

A.B. YEHOSHUA, MAR MANI
Mr. Mani

AUGUSTA VICTORIA HOSPITAL, MOUNT SCOPUS (FORMERLY A GERMAN HOSPICE)
named after the wife of Kaiser Wilhelm II of Germany, who visited in Jerusalem in 1898
and built the hospital for German Pilgrims

NEBI SAMWIL (the Prophet Samuel in Arabic)
The building was erected on the 16th century over a burial cave believed to be the tomb of the prophet Samuel.

MONASTERY OF THE CROSS a Greek Orthodox monastery, built on the site where by legend the tree used for the cross grew
The monastery was built in the 12th century. It was built like a fortress, to protect the building against marauding robber bands.

MAR (SAINT) ELIAS MONASTERY ON THE ROAD BETWEEN BETHLEHEM AND JERUSALEM

according to tradition, the monastery, which was built like a fortress, was constructed in a place where the prophet Elijah slept

on his flight from Queen Jezebel (Kings I 19:23)

THE PLACE OF ASCENSION, MOUNT OF OLIVES

according to Christian tradition Jesus ascended into heaven from here

CARMELITE CONVENT, MCUNT OF OLIVES

CHURCH OF OUR LADY OF THE ARK OF THE COVENANT, ABU GHOSH

where by tradition the Ark of the Covenant was brought

CHURCH OF ST. JOHN THE BAPTIST, EIN KAREM

built on what is reputed to be the site of the home of John's parents

RUSSIAN CONVENT "MOSKOVIA," EIN KAREM

CHURCH OF THE VISITATION, EIN KAREM, where by Christian tradition Mary felt Jesus stirring in her womb.

. . . And the walls.

Every quarter, every suburb harbours a hidden kernel surrounded by high walls. Can one ever feel home here in Jerusalem, I wonder, even if one lives here a century? City of enclosed courtyards, her soul sealed up behind bleak walls crowned with jagged glass. There is no Jerusalem. Crumbs have been dropped deliberately to mislead innocent people. There are shells within shells and the kernel is forbidden.

I have written "I was born in Jerusalem"; "Jerusalem is my city," this I cannot write. I cannot know what lurks in wait for me in the depths of the Russian Compound, behind the walls of the Schneller Barracks, in the monastic lairs of Ein Kerem or in the enclave of the High Commisioner's Palace on the Hill of Evil Council. This is a brooding city.

AMOS OZ, MICHA'EL SHELI
My Michael

CHURCH OF THE VISITATION, EIN KAREM

MARY'S TOMB, CHURCH OF THE ASSUMPTION

according to Christian tradition, Mary is believed to have been buried here

CHURCH OF ALL NATIONS The church owes its name to the fact that
men of all nations contributed to its construction, also known as
CHURCH OF THE AGONY (GETHSEMANE), MOUNT OF OLIVES.

THE UNFINISHED CHURCH, EIN KAREM

. . . A few moments brought us to the crest of the hill Scopus, whence Titus and the Crusaders had gazed on the devoted city with very different emotions. In the first sight of Jerusalem there is a thrill of interest which is scarcely weakened by repetition, and one can only pity the man who is not, for the moment at least, imbued with the pilgrim spirit, and does not feel the sight to be one of the privileges of his life. Enshrined in the Christian's affections, linked with every feeling of faith and hope – "If I forget thee, O Jerusalem, let my right hand forget her cunning." I had already in previous years approached Jerusalem from the west, south and east; this was the first occasion on which we had looked at it from the north. On this side there is nothing to excite the feelings; if the mind were not absorbed in the associations evoked by those grey hills which enclosed the little foreground in front, perhaps a sense of disappointment would steal over us. There is but one true approach to Jerusalem, and, if possible, even at the cost of some hours' detour, let the pilgrim endeavour to enter from the east, the favorite approach of our Lord, the path of his last and triumphant entry. It is a glorious burst, as the traveller rounds the shoulder of Mount Olivet, and the Haram wall starts up before him from the deep gorge of the Kedron, with its domes and crescents sparkling in the sunlight – a royal city. On that very spot he (i.e., Jesus) once paused and gazed on the same bold cliffs supporting a far more glorious pile, and when he beheld the city he wept over it.

HENRY BAKER TRISTRAM, TRAVELS IN PALESTINE, DIARY, 1863-1864

CHURCH OF MARY MAGDALENE (RUSSIAN), MOUNT OF OLIVES
The church with seven onion domes was built by Czar Alexander III in 1865,
and it offers one of the most impressive views of Jerusalem

ST. ANDREW CHURCH (SCOTTISH), NEAR THE CINEMATHEQUE

near the Valley of Ben Hinnom

ST. PETER IN GALLICANTU CHURCH ON THE EASTERN SLOPES OF MOUNT ZION,
where by Christian tradition Peter heard a cock crow

ST. ONUPHRIUS (a 4th century Egyptian Christian hermit) MONASTERY, (Aceldama) WHERE THE VALLEY OF BEN HINNOM MEETS THE KIDRON

. . . Suddenly, we stood opposite this incredible city, the divided city, the united city, Jerusalem of which there is no second. Now, it seemed as if all the days and years had been erased, with only the generations preserved there in the stone and marble and in the ruins and remnants.

The first time Jerusalem is mentioned is in the writings of the Egyptians in 2375 B.C.E. ... King David captured it and made it the capital of his kingdom, 1000 B.C.E. ... The armies of Babylon destroyed Jerusalem, 587 B.C.E. ... The building of the Second Temple, 518 B.C.E. ... Antiochus king of Syria ruled over Jerusalem, 170 B.C.E. ... The Maccabees conquered Jerusalem, 165 B.C.E. ... The Roman armies entered Jerusalem, 63 B.C.E. ... The destruction of Jerusalem and its Temple by Rome, 70 C.E.

And afterwards, after Rome, the rule of the Byzantine Christians, and afterwards Jerusalem was conquered by the Persians, with the aid of the Jews, and afterwards the Byzantines returned to it, and afterwards it fell to the Arabs and their caliph, Ibn Hattab, who was replaced by the caliphs of the Abbas dynasty, and afterwards the Egyptian Ahmad ibn Tulun ruled it, and afterwards it was captured by the caliphs of the Fatimid dynasty, and after them the Seljuks and again the Fatimids, and afterwards the Crusaders invaded Jerusalem. And it was but the year 1099, and soon there would arrive the traveller Binyamin of Tudela in 1173, and after him the Muslims led by their king, Saladin, 1187, and some time after this three hundred rabbis arrived from England and France. But afterwards the Mongols (Tatars) destroyed it in 1260, and then the Muslim Mameluks arrived from Egypt and rebuilt it and Nahmanides came and restored the Jewish settlement in Jerusalem. Time passed, and in 1517 the Turks conquered it and approximately two hundred years passed and Rabbi Yehudah Hasid arrived with his disciples, and again there was an Egyptian conquest, by Muhammad Ali, and the first Hebrew book was printed in Jerusalem: Avodat HaKodesh, and the first Hebrew paper, HaLevanon, appeared in Jerusalem in 1863, and now it is as if the way had been opened: Dr. Herzl came through its gates in 1898. The new era: the British in Jerusalem, 1917. The new era, Jerusalem capital of Israel, about 3,000 years after King David established his monarchy in it.

Good God! What has this city not endured, and here it is before us right now, in the setting light of the sun.

SAUL BELLOW, TO JERUSALEM AND BACK

CITY OF DAVID, THE KIDRON VALLEY AND THE SHILOAH (SILOAM) POOL,
one of the important water sources of ancient Jerusalem

A SECTION OF THE SOUTHERN WALL OF THE OLD CITY

GOLDEN GATE

There were seven gates in the wall of Jerusalem

And they did not know through which to enter

For each gate jumped and danced before them, saying

Come through me, for I am most worthy to you of all.

The Holy One, blessed be He, sat in the Court on High

And the Ministering Angels to His Right and Left.

He said to them,

Which gate is worthy that the redemption may come by it?

For two angels do not perform a single task

And two gates do not bring a single deliverance.

And they did not know what to answer Him!

Michael arose and said, Lord of the Universe!

All are precious and all are worthy.

Rather call the gates and let them press their cases before You

And You will choose one of them.

The Holy One, blessed be He, said

I swear, that that is what I will do!

YITZHAK NAVON, SHESHET HAYAMIM VESHIVAT HASHE'ARIM
(The Six Days and the Seven Gates)

The Mercy (Golden) Gate (Bab el Rahmeh) appears in the legends of all three religions. An early Jewish
tradition holds that it is through this gate that the Messiah will enter Jerusalem.
According to Christian tradition, Jesus made his last entry into Jerusalem through the Mercy Gate.
The Muslims refer to it as the Gate of Mercy and believe it to be the gate referred to in the Koran,
through which the just will pass on the Day of Judgment.

For me, the roof of Notre Dame was like Mt. Nevo so high,
I'd see the sacred place, unable to draw nigh.

Pallid dots yonder on the Mt. of Olives,
tombstones, my brother, and beneath, the dead in graves.

They didn't dwell in our thoughts for five long years
we didn't pray in their homes or their graves wreath with tears.
And it's all so near... take them, stretch out your hands –
the Jaffa Gate and the Damascus Gate where it stands.

And it's all so far, as a fleeting dream leaves you bare
You've come down from the roof – they're no longer there.

Just a kind of sensation at your finger tips
Just choking back tears... and a clenching of lips.

YITZHAK SHALEV, AL GAG HANOTER DAM
(From the Roof of Notre Dame)
Translated by Aloma Halter

A VIEW FROM THE NOTRE DAME MONASTERY TOWARD THE NEW CITY
Notre Dame, formerly a Hospice, is now a hotel for Christian pilgrims

A VIEW FROM THE NOTRE DAME MONASTERY
TOWARD THE OLD CITY

ST. SALVATORE, FRANCISCAN MONASTERY ADJACENT TO THE OLD CITY WALL

CHURCH OF THE HOLY SEPULCHER, AND THE BELL TOWER OF THE CHURCH OF THE REDEEMER (LUTHERAN)

THE MURISTAN (Persian for "Hospital"). The hospital was built during the
Crusader era and deserted in the 16th century,
CHURCH OF THE HOLY SEPULCHER AND CHURCH OF THE REDEEMER

DOME OF THE CHURCH OF THE HOLY SEPULCHER
which dates from the time of the Crusaders,
AND THE BELL TOWER OF THE CHURCH OF THE REDEEMER (LUTHERAN)

THE MUSLIM QUARTER

. . . The next day the duke went to the Via Dolorosa, and, at the behest of his forefathers, who had been Knights-Templars, walked from the Praetorium to the Church of the Holy Sepulcher with his eyes closed, surrounded by guards and others who prevented him from colliding with the stone walls.

At the Fourth Station he placed the palms of his hands on the imprint of the Virgin's feet in the "sandal mosaic" and began trembling violently.

At the Sixth Station he burst into tears, and at the Station of St. Veronica the priests brought out her white silk kerchief to wipe the tears, sweat and blood from his face. Throughout that time the duke did not open his eyes, but when he returned to his tent he ordered the photographer to photograph the path he had followed until that point.

"Take a pace and snap a photograph, another and again a photograph!" he ordered him. He himself went out to the slopes of Mount Scopus, where he was shown a jumble of vertebrae and other ribs, teeth and thighbones, like parts of a frightful construction set. It was no longer possible to say who was Pharaoh's daughter here, who was Na'ama the Ammonite, who was Yael the princess of Tadmor, and who was Louisa, the Crusader saint. "The dead," his adviser whispered to him as they left the cave, "are the strongest guild in Jerusalem."

MEIR SHALEV, ESAV
(Esau)

VIA DOLOROSA – The Way of the Cross AND THE SLOPES OF MOUNT SCOPUS AND THE MOUNT OF OLIVES

. . . How beautiful is the commencement of the Sabbath at the Western Wall. The holy rocks, which in their holiness shine forth to us from the darkness of our exile, impart an additional element of sanctity to the sanctity of the Sabbath, with which the holy Israel sanctify themselves, and through whose remembrance and observance they will yet be redeemed. Yitzhak stands and prays either by heart or from the prayer book. Sometimes his heart is drawn by the simple and warm-hearted melodies of the Perushim, and at other times by the tunes of the Hasidim, sometimes by the tunes of the Hasidim who have awe in their hearts, and sometimes by the tunes of those fervent Hasidim whose prayers are a fiery flame. And within each tune there sings in Yitzhak's heart his own tune which is blended with the tune he received from his town.

In his great fervor, Yitzhak removes all his sins from his heart and appears to himself as an infant without sin, free of all fault as when he had been a child among the children in his town – with the added sanctity of the Sabbath in Jerusalem. How beautiful is the light of mercy to a soul which yearns.

S.Y. AGNON, T'MOL SHILSHOM
(Yesterday and the Day Before)

THE CARDO a major street originally built in Roman and Byzantine Periods,
AND THE HURVAH SYNAGOGUE, built in 1864 and destroyed by the
Jordanians after the fall of the Old City in 1948. THE JEWISH QUARTER

THE WESTERN WALL PLAZA AND YESHIVAT HAKOTEL

THE JEWISH QUARTER AND THE WESTERN WALL PLAZA, LOOKING NORTH

. . . Suddenly the cry goes out:

"There's the Wall! There's the Wall!"

They come to a halt. To the right is an enormous wall. Massive, gray rocks.

The Western Wall.

All gaze. The Western Wall! It's the Western Wall!

They gaze at the high wall. Large rocks with moss. The Prayer Wall. The Wall of Tears.

They dream . . .

MOTA GUR, HAR HABAYIT BEYADEINU
(The Temple Mount is in our Hands)

THE JEWISH QUARTER AND THE WESTERN WALL PLAZA

. . . The mighty Mosque of Omar and the paved court around it occupy a fourth part of Jerusalem. They are upon Mount Moriah, where King Solomon's Temple stood. This mosque is the holiest place the Muhammedan knows outside of Mecca. Up to within a year or two past, no Christian could gain admission to it or its court for love or money. But the prohibition has been removed, and we entered freely for baksheesh.

I need not speak of the wonderful beauty and the exquisite grace and symmetry that have made this mosque so celebrated – because I did not see them. One cannot see such things at an instant glance – one frequently only finds out how really beautiful a beautiful woman is after considerable acquaintance with her; and the rule applies to Niagara Falls, to majestic mountains, and to mosques – especially to mosques.

The great feature of the Mosque of Omar is the prodigious rock in the center of its rotunda. It was upon this rock that Abraham came so near to offering his son Isaac, this, at least, is authentic – it is very much more to be relied on than most of the traditions, at any rate. On this rock also the angel stood and threatened Jerusalem, and David persuaded him to spare the city. Muhammad was well acquainted with this stone. From it he ascended to heaven. The stone tried to follow him, and if the angel Gabriel had not happened by the merest good luck to be there to seize it, it would have done it. Very few people have a grip like Gabriel – the prints of his monstrous fingers, two inches deep, are to be seen in that rock today.

MARK TWAIN, THE INNOCENTS ABROAD, 1867

THE TEMPLE MOUNT AND THE WESTERN WALL PLAZA

THE TEMPLE MOUNT, THE DOME OF THE ROCK AND THE AL-AKSA MOSQUE

. . . Filled with anguish, after having toured the land and having seen what I saw in Jaffa and the "colonies" (i.e., the new settlements), I came to Jerusalem just before Passover, to pour out my words and my wrath to "the trees and rocks," the remnants of our most precious site of antiquity.

My first step was, of course, the Wall. There I found some of our brothers, who reside in Jerusalem, standing and praying very loudly. Their emaciated faces, their strange motions and their peculiar clothing – all are in keeping with the terrible appearance of the Wall. I stood looking at them and at the Wall, and a single thought filled all the recesses of my heart: these rocks are witness to the destruction of our land, and these people – to the destruction of our nation; which of the two calamities was the greater? Which one should we mourn for more? – If a land is destroyed but its people are still full of life and vigor – a Zerubabel, Ezra and Nehemiah can arise, followed by the people, and they can return and rebuild it: but if a nation is destroyed, who can arise for it and from whence will its aid come?

Had the spirit of Rabbi Yehudah Halevi come upon me at that time and had I been able to lament, as did he, the destruction of my people, my lament would not have begun with the word "Zion," but with the word "Israel."

AHAD HAAM, LIFNEI HAKOTEL
(Before the Wall)

THE TEMPLE MOUNT, THE DOME OF THE ROCK (built in 691)
AND THE AL-AKSA MOSQUE (first built in the 8th Century)

THE JEWISH QUARTER AND BATEI MAHSEH,
built by Dutch and German Jews in 1858 and destroyed
by the Jordanians. It has been partly rebuilt

THE OLD CITY

. . . Once every twenty-eight years, in the Nissan season, in the early morning hours on a Wednesday, according to the calculations of our ancient astronomers, the sun completes its major cycle and returns to its exact place in the heavens, at exactly the place where it had been placed at the moment of its creation.

. . . While it was still night, at a time where all were still asleep, my great-grandfather would climb, together with his friend, Rabbi Hiyye David Shpitzer – the author of Nivreshet – to the top of the Mount of Olives, and there, close to the Russian Church – which in those days had a large bell in its bell tower, dragged there by rope from the Jaffa port by Russian pilgrims – they would stand, facing the east, and would note down the exact time at which the sun would first begin to appear above the hilltops, the Moabite hills.

At that exact time, their friends would stand on the roof of the Hurvah synagogue and mark down the time of sunrise from where they stood, and this way they were able to calculate how much later sunrise is in Jerusalem itself because of the shadow which the Mount of Olives casts on the city.

HAYYIM BEER, NOTZOT
(Feathers)

DOME OF THE CHURCH OF THE HOLY SEPULCHER AND THE BELL TOWER OF THE CHURCH OF THE REDEEMER

... From the porch of an ancient synagogue we saw, in the radiant light of the morning, the location of the Temple, the Mount of Olives, and the entire legend-saturated landscape. I believe with all my heart that it is possible to establish, outside the old walls of the city, a new, exquisite Jerusalem.

The old Jerusalem will remain a type of Lourdes, Mecca, and "Jerusalem the Holy." An attractive and elegant city can be built in this area.

... In the afternoon we were on the Mount of Olives.

Great moments. How much can be done with this magnificent area. A city such as Rome, and the Mount of Olives can be as beautiful as the Janiculum.

I would take the Old City, along with its saints, and lock them up as if in a crate. I would remove all commerce from it, having only Houses of God and charitable institutions remain within the ancient wall. And on the slopes of the hills in a wide swath around it, which will become green with vegetation by our effort, the exquisite Jerusalem will be located.

On the road which climbs to the Mount of Olives will travel the finest of men from throughout the entire world. A caring hand will transform Jerusalem into a precious jewel. Everything holy will be contained within the ancient walls, while everything new will spread out for a distance around them.

We climbed the Russian Tower, I only to the first level, because I had a dizzy spell; the others went to the top. The view extended to the Jordan Valley and the slopes of its hills, the Dead Sea, the Moabite mountains, and the Eternal City, Jerusalem.

THEODOR HERZL, (DIARIES)

THE GATE OF MERCY, KNOWN AS THE GOLDEN GATE
THROUGH WHICH THE MESSIAH IS BY TRADITION TO APPEAR, AND THE
TEMPLE MOUNT

LIONS' GATE

I have another city in addition to my own

Like blood which has too much wine or too much tar.

A city of great stones and torn bars

Half of it is in rock.

Half of it is flying, gliding, to the sky of the King above it

A glowing light that shines until night.

A city of mountains, my head is elsewhere because of it,

It falls to the valley

Faints there and

Breaks up into pieces.

Leaps up

Up and up in the solitude of its towers

In love with the sky.

A yearning city, another city

Built of muffled cries.

I have a city, a wound.

HAIM GURI, IR PETZA
(Wound City)

Known in Hebrew as the Lions' Gate. Legend has it that the lions engraved on both sides of the gate
were placed there by the Ottoman Sultan Suleiman the Magnificent, because he had dreamed that he
would be devoured by lions unless he built a wall around the Holy City for the defense of its citizens.

. . . The Great Khan has an atlas whose drawings depict the earth, all in one and each continent separately, including the borders of the remotest kingdoms, the sea routes, the length of the shores, the largest and most famous cities and the richest ports.

. . . Beside each city, as beside Laudomia, is a city whose inhabitants all have the same name. This is Laudomia-of-the- Dead, the cemetery. But the uniqueness of Laudomia is that it is not merely doubled, but tripled, that is, it also includes Laudomia the Third, the city of those who have not yet been born.

The characteristics of the double city are well known. The more Laudomia-of-the-Living becomes populated and grows larger, the more the area of the graves beyond the walls grows. The streets of Laudomia-of-the-Dead are only as wide as is necessary for the passage of the gravediggers' cart, and many windowless buildings look out on them, but the plan of the streets and the arrangement of the houses is the same as in Laudomia-of-the- Living, and in both the families are crowded together in burial caves, one next to the other. In the afternoon hours on sunny days, the living inhabitants come to visit the dead and identify their names on the gravestones: and like the living city, this city also tells a story of labor, annoyance, illusions, feelings, except that here everything has changed to what is essential and vital, not merely the inconsequential. Everything here is integrated and arranged as it should be. In order to feel secure, Laudomia-of-the-Living must search for its own meaning in Laudomia-of-the-Dead, despite the danger of finding more or less than it intended, i.e., more than one Laudomia, or various cities that could have been and weren't, or to find partial, contradictory or disappointing reasons.

Rightfully, Laudomia also sets aside housing space of similar size for those who have not yet been born. Naturally, the area allotted them is not yet directly proportionate to their number, since it is assumed to be infinitely large. But life in that place is completely empty, surrounded by structures that are but niches and hollows and cracks ... In one small segment of marble we can see all of Laudomia as it will look in another hundred or thousand years from today, brimming entirely with crowds of people wearing garments that no one has ever seen before.

ITALO CALVINO, HEARIM HASEMUYOT MEIAYIN
(The Cities Hidden from the Eye)

CHURCH OF THE ASCENSION (RUSSIAN), MOUNT OF OLIVES. The site is identified as the place where Jesus ascended to heaven.

CHURCH OF THE ASCENSION (RUSSIAN), MOUNT OF OLIVES

147

. . . The Italian archaeologist, Ermata Pierotti, poet, historian, architect and orphan, wrote in his "Ancient Graves in Northern Jerusalem", that one night, on February 27, 1856, a wind blew in from the desert, coating all the gardens of Jerusalem with a thin mixture of sand and salt. There was mass confusion. Even the oldest inhabitants of the city could not recall such a strange storm. That night no one slept, and the next day, in the area between the burial places of the kings and the Europeos mosaic, Pierotti's workers uncovered a small grave with a single word inscribed on it, "Mother."

Pierotti began trembling. He was seized by a strange desire: to fall down and lay his head on the grave, but he was a scientist, and he tried to regain his composure. He had never heard of such an inscription. He was used to finding tombstones which had been decorated and which contained all types of praises for the deceased, yet here was a grave without even a name or any other identifying mark. Had it not had the word "Mother" on it, one might have thought it was the grave of a child, because the residents of Jerusalem did not write the names of children on their graves. As he stood amazed, a wave of pain coursed through his thighs and forced him to fall to the ground. His head struck the tombstone and he almost fainted. With power beyond what he believed he was capable of, he drew his lips closer to the inscription and blew away from it the grains of sand inside the inscription. As he did so, his eyes were filled with the salty earth and with tears. A great trembling passed through the air, issuing a sound like taut wires just before a storm.

. . . One man left the crowd and came over, and after him another and then another, and soon a whole pile of small orphaned stones was formed on the tombstone. Pierotti, too, placed a stone on it and he, too, backed away, refusing to go back to the tombstone in order to expose and study it, even though a larcenous impulse drove him to break in to the grave, to touch the bones ... After all, who among us did not love his mother, and who did not leave her behind, forsaken, lying down and sobbing? And who did not wrong her?

MEIR SHALEV, ESAV
(Esau)

THE MUSLIM CEMETERY ADJACENT TO THE LIONS' GATE
Muslim tradition has it that this will be the site of the resurrection of
the dead in the end of days

THE JEWISH CEMETERY ON THE MOUNT OF OLIVES
By Jewish tradition, the Final Redemption will take place here.

HAR HA-MENUHOT ("HILL OF REPOSE") CEMETERY

near the western entrance to Jerusalem

THE WORLD WAR I BRITISH MILITARY CEMETERY

ON MOUNT SCOPUS

. . . I saw the Jewish people according to its communities and groupings, with their customs, apart and together, the weeping women near David's Tomb and the dark vaults with the smoke from the flickering candles. So too did I see many tourists with straw hats and cameras, standing next to the mourners or those who cried and prayed with them; and I saw young men who, based on their appearance, belong to the basketball team of this or that college, and in their eyes one could sense the grief of Jerusalem the destroyed.

And I saw family after family ascending the mountain slowly and waiting for a tired grandmother or for a grandfather leaning on a wall, as well as people carrying children in their arms or on their backs. There were also many beggars there for all types of causes, along the entire road leading up the hill.

There were tour guides from all types of companies, who dragged the non-Jews up so that they could evidently see how this strange nation remembers its destroyed Temple.

From there I went on to the Cellar of the Holocaust and saw those standing silently opposite the memorial candles and between the marble tablets which had been attached to the walls, a memorial for hundreds of communities which had been destroyed "in the years of destruction and killing" and in the years of "the Holocaust and destruction" by "the German Nazis, may there names be blotted out"; a memorial "to the holy and pure and God-fearing," to "fathers and mothers and children and brothers and sisters and friends." "Earth, do not conceal their blood" was engraved there.

And I saw women shedding a tear and a youth leader implanting in the hearts of his kova tembel-wearing group the meaning, and I turned away from there because I couldn't stand the sight of a father showing his children sections of Torah scrolls encrusted with blood, and torn tallitot, which had been gathered and brought here to be displayed in glass cases. And I saw a group of American Jewish tourists, based on the mixture of Yiddish and English, standing for a long time before a row of jars. I went out from there to the Road of the Yellow Star, to the strong, blinding Israeli sun, and I did not know why it was blinding my eyes right then, and I covered my eyes with sunglasses.

HAIM GURI, DAPEI YERUSHALAYIM
(Jerusalem Pages)

GRAVE OF ZECHARIAH AND THE TOMB OF THE PRIESTLY HEZIR FAMILY,
The Hezir family is mentioned in the book of Nehemiah
NAHAL KIDRON

YAD VASHEM, VALLEY OF THE COMMUNITIES,
commemorating the Jewish communities destroyed by the Nazis in
World War II. THE HOLOCAUST MEMORIAL COMPLEX

THE MAIN MILITARY CEMETERY FOR THOSE WHO FELL IN ISRAEL'S WARS, MOUNT HERZL

YAD VASHEM, MOUNT HERZL

155

YAD VASHEM, MOUNT HERZL

HAR HAMENUHOT

VIEW FROM THE KASTEL, a hill dominating the road to Jerusalem.
Crusader Fortress which was used by the Arab armies during the War of
Independence

HAR HAMENUHOT

The main and largest cemetery of Jerusalem

At seven, at seven twenty
They took them
To the Police Academy
All those who had remained
From Ammunition Hill..

Smoke rose up from the hill
The sun climbed high in the east
Seven of us came back to the city
From Ammunition Hill.

Seven returned to the city
Smoke rose up from the hill
The sun climbed high in the east
Over Ammunition Hill.

Over fortified bunkers
Over our brothers, the men
Who remained there aged only twenty
At Ammunition Hill.

YORAM TEHARLEV, GIVAT HATAHMOSHET
(Ammunition Hill)

AMMUNITION HILL,
a former Jordanian stronghold, site of fierce battles in the Six Day War – now a war memorial

As one in whose life Jerusalem is a central element, as one who accompanied his comrades,

who fell on the way to the city, As one who was the Chief of Staff of the IDF soldiers

in their assault to raise up the Israeli flags on the stones of the Walls,

I would wish that, here, in the city which witnessed thousands of years of longing and suffering,

That here the conflicts between us and our enemies will come to an end,

And here in Jerusalem the Golden, peace treaties will be signed.

— — —

YITZHAK RABIN
Address on the Occasion Marking 25 Years of the Liberation of Jerusalem

MEMORIAL CEREMONY AT THE PARATROOPER MONUMENT,
LIONS' GATE, MAY 31, 1992

HEROD'S GATE

Beautiful of Elevation! Joy of the world City of the Great King!

For you my soul is longing from the limits of the west.

The tumult of my tenderness is stirred when I remember

Your glory of old that is departed – your habitation which is desolate.

O that I might fly on eagles' wings,

That I might water your dust with my tears until they mingle together.

I have sought you, even though your King is not in you and though, in place

Of your Gilead's balm, are now the fiery serpent and the scorpion.

Shall I not be tender to your stones and kiss them,

And the taste of your soil is sweeter than honey unto me.

YEHUDAH HALEVI, YEFEH NOF

The first name was given to the gate by pilgrims, who erroneously believed that it led to Herod's palace.
It is also known in Arabic as the Flower Gate.

BLOOMFIELD GARDEN AND LIBERTY BELL GARDEN,
dedicated on the United States Bicentennial

ROSE GARDEN (WOHL PARK), NEAR THE KNESSET

We sought to roll back as soon as we could the humiliating desolation and barrenness inflicted by foreign invaders, from Roman times until the Turkish era, upon the Jerusalem hills.

During the Biblical era and that of the Second Temple they were blanketed with forests and vineyards, and non-fruitbearing trees along with fruit trees covered the slopes and crests of the hills. The terebinth and the oak, the cypress and the cedar, as well as other tree species, along with pomegranates and sweet fruit trees, villages with spikenard and saffron, canna and cinnamon, along with frankincense, myrrh and aloes, and every other spice.

DAVID BEN-GURION, TIFARTA SHEL YERUSHALAYIM
(The Glory of Jerusalem)

SHEROVER PROMENADE, EAST TALPIOT

THE HAAS PROMENADE AND EAST TALFIOT south east of Jerusalem

169

Doves two

To Jerusalem flew.

– What did they eat?

Grains of light.

What did they drink?

Water of the well.

– Where did they sleep?

On a high wall.

– And what did they dream?

Israel has risen!

Doves two

Returned to Jerusalem.

– What did they tell?

Grew, grew, grew!

There stands a Wall,

There stands a door,

And the Israelites

Sing a song

Next year

Will the city be built.

LEVIN KIPNIS, YONIM SHTAYIM
(Doves Two)

ORDE WINGATE (SALAMEH) SQUARE, TALBIEH

BLOOMFIELD GARDEN AND YEMIN MOSHE,

the latter founded in 1892, is an Artists Quarter

CINEMATHEQUE BRIDGE, HEBRON ROAD

MALHA BRIDGE, GOLOMB STREET

Jerusalem is a port city on the banks of Eternity.

The Temple Mount is a large ship, a luxurious pleasure cruiser.

From the portholes of its Western Wall the pious

light-hearted travellers peer out. Hasidim on the wharf wave Goodbye,

shout Hurray, See you soon. It

Always arrives, always sails. And the fences and the piers

And the policemen and the flags and the tall spires of the churches

And the mosques and the chimneys of the synagogues and the boats

Of praise and the waves of the hills. The sound of a shofar is heard: Another one

Has sailed away. The Yom Kippur sailors in their white uniforms

Climb between the ladders and ropes of tested prayers.

And the give and take and the gates and the golden domes:

Jerusalem is God's Venice.

YEHUDAH AMIHAI,
Poem 21 of a series on Jerusalem, 1967

"STEPS," A STATUE BY EZRA ORION, HERZOG BOULEVARD

ALLENBY PLAZA, ROMEMA, where the Turks surrendered to the British.

The monument commemorating the capture of Jerusalem in 1917 by British troops under General Allenby

A true story in Jerusalem the city / of a monster old and a boy itty-bitty

And it's all true and clear as the sun / without shadow of falsehood – that isn't done

But before I dip my pen in the well / about the monster I first would tell:

A gigantic creature imagine if you can / as the serpent of legend and Og of Bashan

Fire and smoke gush forth from its lips / scales on its hide and its tail a whip

Each of its claws the size of an oar / two hundred its teeth, yellow and hard to the core

Its bones as a rock thick and dense / but simple and modest without demand or offense

Shy and hiding among the hills and streams / larger than life, but dreamer of dreams.

MEIR SHALEV, HAYELED HAYYIM VEHAMIFLETZET MIYERUSHALAYIM
(The Child Hayyim and the Monster from Jerusalem)
Translated by Shmuel Himelstein

(JOHN F.) KENNEDY MEMORIAL, built in 1966 with funds from American Jewish Donors.

The memorial was built in the shape of a tree stump whose roots spread onto a paved square.

The stump expresses how Kennedy's plans were brought to a halt by his assassination.

SHEROVER PROMENADE, CENTRAL SECTION

ROCKEFELLER MUSEUM
The first archaeological museum in Israel, which was built by a donation of the American John D. Rockefeller.
Opened in 1938, it contains Middle Eastern antiquities, mainly found in excavation in Palestine
prior to the establishment of the State of Israel

THE TEMPLE MOUNT, OR MOUNT MORIAH

On the day when, according to Jewish tradition Abraham ascended Mount Moriah to sacrifice Isaac,

the city of Jerusalem had already been in existence for about a thousand years.

Here stood the First Temple; here stood the Second Temple and here the Muslims built their Dome of the Rock.

Above: A PARK NEAR DAVID'S TOWER, attributed to King David; rebuilt by King Herod

Below: ISRAEL MUSEUM, JERUSALEM

JERUSALEM DAY PARADE, MAY 31, 1992, HEROD'S GATE

DAMASCUS GATE

... A fast walker could go outside the walls of Jerusalem and walk entirely around the city in an hour. I do not know how else to make one understand how small it is. The appearance of the city is peculiar. It is as knobby with countless little domes as a prison door is with bolt heads. Every house has from one to half a dozen of these white plastered domes of stone, broad and low, sitting in the center of or in a cluster upon the flat roof. Wherefore, when one looks down from an eminence upon the compact mass of houses (so closely crowded together, in fact, that there is no appearance of streets at all, and so the city looks solid), he sees the knobbiest town in the world, except Constantinople. It looks as if it might be roofed, from center to circumference, with inverted saucers. The monotony of the view is interrupted only by the great Mosque of Omar, the Tower of Hippicus, and one or two other buildings that rise into commanding prominence.

The houses are generally two stories high, built strongly of masonry, whitewashed or plastered outside, and have a cage of wooden latticework projecting in front of every window. To reproduce a Jerusalem street, it would only be necessary to up-end a chicken coop and hang it before each window in an alley of American houses.

The streets are roughly and badly paved with stone, and are tolerably crooked – enough so to make each street appear to close together constantly and come to an end about a hundred yards ahead of the pilgrim as long as he chooses to walk in it. Projecting from the top of the lower story of many of the houses is a very narrow porch roof, or shed, without supports from below; and I have several times seen cats jump across the street from one shed to the other when they were out calling. The cats could have jumped double the distance without extraordinary exertion. I mention these things to give an idea of how narrow the streets are. Since a cat can jump across them without the least inconvenience, it is hardly necessary to state that such streets are too narrow for carriages. These vehicles cannot negotiate the Holy City.

MARK TWAIN, THE INNOCENTS ABROAD, 1867

The most massive and ornate of all of Jerusalem's gates. The road running off it leads on to Shechem (Nablus) and then to Damascus.

On the left: RESIDENTIAL AREA IN GILO, a new neighborhood south of Jerusalem begun in 1970.

On the right: DAMASCUS GATE AND THE OLD CITY,

the road from this gate leads (via Nablus) to Damascus. In Hebrew it is known as SHA'AR SHECHEM, the Nablus Gate

. . . Avigdor stood on the roof of his home and gazed at the city. House touching house and roof to roof. A person is able to move from the one end of Jerusalem to the other by means of the roofs of its houses. It is like a city compacted together, Avigdor read in the language of the Psalms, and he gave a deep, bitter sigh. Jerusalem is joined together by its houses and divided by its residents. What caused you, O Jerusalem, to become like that?

S.Y. AGNON, KENAGAN HAMENAGEN
(As a Musician Playing)

THE ENTRANCE TO A RESIDENTIAL COMPLEX IN GILO

After the Temple was destroyed, the Sages – the leaders of the generation – decreed that one must show distress over the destruction from that time on in the lives of the Children of Israel.

If a person plasters his home with plaster, he leaves unplastered a cubit by a cubit opposite the front door ...

So too did they decree that a person who provides a meal for guests should leave out some little item and leave an open place without one of the plates which should be placed there. And when a woman wears gold or silver jewelry, she should leave out one item which she would normally wear so that her jewelry should not be complete.

And all of these are in order to remember Jerusalem, as it states, "If I forget you, O Jerusalem, may my right hand forget its cunning, may my tongue cleave to the roof of my month should I not remember you; should I not mention Jerusalem as my chief joy" (Ps. 137).

MAIMONIDES, LAWS OF FASTS, 8:12-13

SHMUEL HANAVI NEIGHBORHOOD,

DAMASCUS GATE – LOOKING FROM THE OLD CITY

up to 1967, this area was on the border of Jordanian-held Jerusalem

RAMOT, LOOKING SOUTH

GILO, LOOKING NORTH

MA'ALEH ADUMIM

194

GIVAT HAMIVTAR, a new neighborhood, built in 1970

THE "BUILD YOUR OWN HOME" SECTION, RAMOT

RAMOT ESHKOL (founded 1969)
AND MAALOT DAFNA (founded 1972)

MORNING FOG IN RAMOT, a neighborhood

In the mornings of winter

The valleys of Jerusalem are permeated

With a gray fog,

Which surrounds the walls,

Turrets and towers

Like a nest about a bird.

And one who drives on the road

Around the wall prays silently,

May it be that in this fog

I do not meet anyone

I do not hit anyone,

That we may pass through the gray sea

And arrive in peace

At the illuminated shore

Of the morning sun

of Abu-Tor.

YEHOASH BIBBER, ARAFEL BOKER YERUSHALAYIM
(Morning Fog Jerusalem)

RAMOT ESHKOL

RESIDENTIAL AREA IN EAST TALPIOT, (founded 1972)

JERUSALEM DAY MARCH, MAY 31, 1992, DAMASCUS GATE

The Jerusalem March is in a way akin to the pilgrimages of the Jewish people to Jerusalem during the Temple eras

DAMASCUS GATE STEPS

JERUSALEM DAY MARCH, MAY 31, 1992, DAMASCUS GATE

 NEW GATE

. . . We are all united in our love for Jerusalem. However the test of a city is in deed.
The largest city in the State is faced with great tasks, and one of the most important of
these is absorbing immigrants on a large scale. We are at present in the process of
implementing large economic projects which can give the city renewed momentum.

. . . Perspicacity and sensitivity are the key to our sovereignty in Jerusalem.
The world, whose eyes are focused on Jerusalem, will measure us according to the way
we relate to the minority living among us.

Today, on this day, the State of Israel can be proud of the freedom of religion
and the scrupulous care of the holy places which we have in Jerusalem, the capital of Israel.

FROM A SPEECH BY TEDDY KOLLEK, NOVEMBER 4, 1992

This is little more than an opening in the wall – wide enough to take motor traffic. It was constructed in
1887 by Sultan Abdul Hamid to provide easy access to the Christian Quarter of the Old City from the
developing new northern suburbs outside the walls.

ISRAEL MUSEUM, JERUSALEM, including an Art Museum, Biblical and
Archaeological Museum, Sculpture Museum, The Shrine of the Book, and
changing exhibits

SUPREME COURT, JANUARY 1992

SUPREME COURT, NOVEMBER 1992

ISRAEL MUSEUM, JERUSALEM

ISRAEL MUSEUM, JERUSALEM

THE NEWLY OPENED BIELE LANDS MUSEUM

SHRINE OF THE BOOK, ISRAEL MUSEUM, JERUSALEM, WHICH FEATURES AN EXHIBIT OF THE DEAD SEA SCROLLS

ISRAEL MUSEUM, JERUSALEM, ENTRANCE TO YOUTH WING

BILLY ROSE ART GARDEN

ISRAEL MUSEUM, JERUSALEM

ENTRANCE DRIVEWAY TO THE HYATT HOTEL

SPORT CENTER, HEBREW UNIVERSITY, GIVAT RAM CAMPUS

BELGIUM HOUSE, HEBREW UNIVERSITY, GIVAT RAM CAMPUS

TEDDY (KOLLEK) STADIUM, MALHA, JERUSALEM'S NEW SPORT STADIUM

... As we entered the Teddy Stadium, we remembered the good old days of the YMCA stadium. There you had nothing to look forward to. Here, at this five million dollar stadium, you leave your car at the Golden Gate and go to the entrance gate.

Do you wish to enter? Do you know the password? All the entrances are sealed off by police barricades, and people crawl through as if into solitary confinement cells. The beloved horses have left the stables. In YMCA they would graze on the grass at the sides of the playing field. In the Teddy Stadium they forage about looking for dandruff in the people's heads.

... That was the first meeting of the season between two similar cultures, two similar populations. Many young people, lots of enthusiasm, color, imagination and a "wild" crowd.
Ever since the Betar team had received the Teddy Stadium, there had never been so large a foreign crowd, which threatened Betar's control of the bleachers. The Bnei Yehudah crowd was dominant before the kick-off, while those of Betar, somewhat taken aback by their vocal inferiority, responded with ear-splitting catcalls.

AVIAD FORHELES, SPORT COLUMN, YEDI'OT AHARONOT, NOVEMBER 15, 1992

TEDDY STADIUM, MALHA, NOVEMBER, 14, 1992

THE KNESSET, ISRAEL'S PARLIAMENT

CENTER 1 SHOPPING CENTER AND THE JERUSALEM GATE HOTEL,
AT THE ENTRANCE TO JERUSALEM

THE MORMON CENTER, MOUNT SCOPUS

HEBREW UNIVERSITY, MOUNT SCOPUS CAMPUS

THE HYATT HOTEL

HADASSAH HOSPITAL, EIN KEREM,

opened after the hospital on Mount Scopus fell into Jordanian hands in 1948

... The true glory of Jerusalem will not be in monuments to the great people of the past, but in the cultivation of the immortal spirit of the nation — in every branch of the Torah and learning and research, in the establishment of institutions of education and prayer and science which will make Jerusalem the center of wisdom and culture of the Jewish people and the source of spiritual inspiration, as befits the People of the Book.

... Jerusalem has been designated by Divine Providence to be the center of learning, science and the spirit in Israel, not only in the State of Israel but in the entire nation of Israel.

DAVID BEN-GURION, TIFARTA SHEL YERUSHALAYIM
(The Glory of Jerusalem)

HEBREW UNIVERSITY, MOUNT SCOPUS CAMPUS

HEBREW UNIVERSITY, MOUNT SCOPUS CAMPUS

NEW GATE AND THE WALL OF THE OLD CITY. The New Gate was constructed in 1887

. . . I must admit that I have never heard an excessively raised voice, a jarring sound in Jerusalem, neither in its streets, nor in its houses or its mansions. Thus one hears more clearly how God breathes. Staggered at His great closeness, one is overcome with fear and trembling. One must become accustomed to God. It is only proper that one purify oneself, that one always improves. The soul is seized by a deep sense of awe, it begins to blaze. Sometimes I would deliberately hide myself from God.

Not all those who travel to Eretz Israel live there with the full awareness of their mission. Eretz Israel makes demands!!! In order to be healed – and I refer here to the spiritual – Jerusalem, the capital of Eretz Israel, is the right place, the healing spa for the soul, for the city imparts blessing upon the person whose soul seeks it. The city, filled with awe of God, consoles those who seek consolation.

Jerusalem is the spyglass pointing at the World to Come, the heavenly opening of the heavens.

ELSA LASKER-SCHUELLER, JERUSALEM

CLOSING GATE

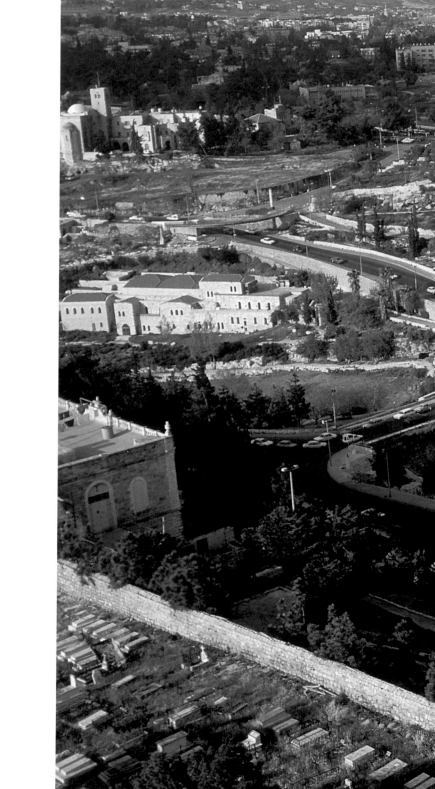

Again the quiet light falls here from evening skies
Like a gliding kite from above deep halls
And a red beam kisses, a sword ablaze,
summits, towers and walls.

I saw a city donning light
And rising in all the rainbow's hues
Ringing in me like a ten-string harp
I saw a city donning light.

And now the shade creeps down from hills of pine
Drawing near the houses, softly, like a lover
Greeted by winks, a myriad eyes of light shine
Suddening opening to me, as if aquiver.

In the stillness of the last watch the city's breathing
And in the velvet skies a last speck pales to white;
It's only dawn, but its golden dome is reddening
To the warm soft touch of new light.

YOSEF SARIG, OR VIRUSHALAYIM
(Light and Jerusalem)
Translated by Richard Flantz

A VIEW FROM THE WALL OF THE OLD CITY
TO YEMIN MOSHE AND THE NEW CITY

We'll return to the songs
and to the heart's voice,
we'll return to measure out
the streets of Jerusalem
with a spool of love's thread.

Even a brief parting
from these stones
leaves behind a hollowness
of sorrowful longing
of absence
which does not return.

Henbane springs into bloom
from the stone courses of Suleiman's walls,
so let's get drunk
and not on wine,
we'll circle around the old walls
seventy seven times.

Even after parting
Jerusalem still remains -
the city is concealed, serene,
patiently waiting
for the two of us together
with fingers interlaced,
to unsheathe from it
skin after skin.

YEHOASH BIBER, AHAREI PREIDAH
(After Parting)
Translated by Aloma Halter